FARM HOUSES THE NEW STYLE

FARM HOUSES THE NEW STYLE

COLLINS|DESIGN
An Imprint of HarperCollinsPublishers

NEILL HEATH

First Edition

First published in 2005 by:
Collins Design
*An Imprint o*f HarperCollins*Publishers*
10 East 53rd Street
New York, New York 10022-5299
Tel: (212) 207-7000
Fax: (212) 207-7654
collinsdesign@harpercollins.com
www.harpercollins.com

Distributed throughout the world by:
HarperCollins*Publishers*
10 East 53rd Street
New York, NY 10022
Fax: (212) 207-7654

Packaged by:
Grayson Publishing, LLC
James G. Trulove, Publisher
1250 28th Street NW
Washington, DC 20007
(202) 337-1380
jtrulove@aol.com

Design: Agnieszka Stachowicz

Library of Congress Control Number: 2005931350

ISBN 0-06-083329-7
ISBN13 978-0-06-083329-9

Manufactured in China
First printing, 2005
1 2 3 4 5 6 7 8 9 / 06 05 04 03

CONTENTS

INTRODUCTION

Though fully modern both in design and construction, the new farm houses featured in this book have several traits in common. The architects have all strongly tied the houses to a sense of place, in terms of both the physical landscape and, to an extent, the historical past.

Whether a vineyard in California's Napa Valley, a ranch in Texas's rolling Hill Country, a cut-flower farm in Louisiana, or a once-rural village in New England, the settings and locations—colored by local materials, styles, and preferences—define these new farm houses. Local buildings provide the architect with a starting point for each design. For example, vernacular farm buildings along the coast of Northern California inspired another house situated in a forest clearing with distant views of the ocean.

Though there are fewer working farms today than before, some homes serve as primary residences for owners who need room for family and friends and space to pursue special interests and hobbies. These new farm houses actually function as working farms, incorporating barns and outbuildings for machinery and equipment. Not surprisingly, others are weekend retreats for city dwellers seeking a rural setting and a scaled-back routine. All new farm houses, however, are connected to the land, are surrounded by the landscape, and reflect the rural agricultural buildings found in the area.

LEFT: The Rappahannock House in rural Virginia, by McInturff Architects.

ABOVE: The Wagner Residence in North Ferrisburgh, Vermont, by Wagner McCann Studio. LEFT: A Farm House in Louisiana, by Holly & Smith Architects. RIGHT: Bucks County House in Tinicum Township, Pennsylvania, by Donald Billinkoff Architects.

A regional vernacular is often represented. A slightly unconventional house in Vermont was inspired by local "maple sugar shacks", and a house in Mississippi incorporates a "dog trot", a form typical of the rural South.

To create the new farm house, the architects here have looked to local rural structures for reference, often combining elements from barns and other agrarian buildings found in the area. Modest, straightforward materials associated with utilitarian buildings are frequently adapted, including corrugated steel, standing seam metal, cedar shingles, and board-and-batten siding. With other houses, traditional materials and details have been replaced with a spare, rugged aesthetic of poured-in-place concrete, concrete block, and aluminum windows.

Most important, this sense of place and connection to the land are characteristics that resonate strongly with the owners of these new homes. The new farm houses are built by owners who are moved by a rolling landscape, who are returning to the area after many years away, who are planning retirement, or who have land that has been in the family, passed down to now grown children. These are houses that harmonize with the environment.

PROJECTS

Rivera Barn

ARCHITECT DAHLIN GROUP ARCHITECTURE PLANNING
LOCATION NAPA VALLEY, CALIFORNIA

The owners of this small retreat in the Napa Valley wanted a quiet getaway from a busy life in San Francisco. The owners, architect, and landscape architect worked together to design the Rivera Barn for simple weekends, guests, or entertaining.

The house overlooks a working vineyard and is surrounded by 65 acres of rolling, brush-covered hills. Less than 1,000 square feet, it is an uncomplicated, warm structure that relates to the setting and the working buildings of the Napa Valley, with some added amenities. The cedar, board-and-batten siding is stained to match the bark of the manzanita trees that cover the hillside. Glazed barn doors open half the length of the building onto a trellis-covered terrace, extending the interior space outside during good weather. A standing seam metal roof reflects the vertical lines of the siding and adds to the simplicity of the building, while the carved stone steps end at the vineyard.

The large, flexible interior space is divided only by the wall at the bath. The bed is tucked behind a buffet on a raised mahogany platform, creating a sense of privacy, yet still allowing a view through the massive glass doors. Ten foot walls are paneled in mahogany. The surface above is sandblasted and is stained cedar as a reminder of the building's rural surroundings.

The interior design features include stained concrete floors, mahogany panels, and a large fireplace. Limestone and zinc countertops reflect a simple palette.

The structure is at the head of a series of outdoor spaces. The walkway is the spine of the plan. From the house, a path meanders past gardens and wildflowers planted among the rocks, through a grove of olive trees, to a spot with an open view of the Napa Valley.

PHOTOGRAPHER DAVID DUNCAN LIVINGSTON

FLOOR PLAN

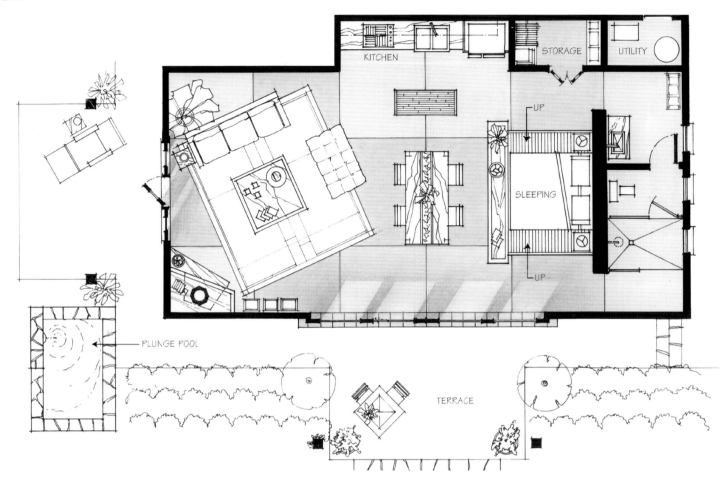

KITCHEN

STORAGE   UTILITY

UP

SLEEPING

UP

PLUNGE POOL

TERRACE

SITE PLAN

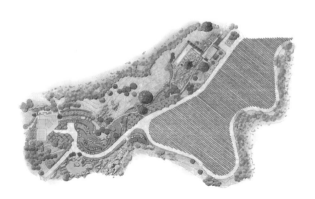

CONCEPT SKETCH

PREVIOUS PAGES: Designed as a retreat for a Bay Area family rather than being planned for guests or entertaining, the house is an uncomplicated structure that relates to the setting and the working buildings of the Napa Valley. ABOVE AND RIGHT: Overlooking a 10 acre vineyard, the house is surrounded by 65 acres of rolling terrain. The cedar board-and-batten siding is stained to match the bark of the manzanita trees that cover the hillside. A vineyard forms the front yard.

LEFT: A trellis-covered gravel terrace runs the length of the house. Large barn doors open during good weather, merging the interior with the outside. ABOVE: The interior space is large, open, and flexible. A single interior wall separates the bath. Mahogany panels cover the walls to a height of 10 feet. Above, the wall surface is sandblasted, stained cedar, a reminder of the building's rural surroundings.

ABOVE LEFT: The interior is straightforward and features stained concrete floors, mahogany panels, and a large fireplace.
ABOVE: Glazed barn doors open half the length of the building onto a trellis-covered gravel terrace.

ABOVE LEFT: Positioned behind a buffet on a raised mahogany platform, the sleeping area maintains a sense of privacy, yet still enjoys a view through the massive glass doors. ABOVE: The bath is separated from the open plan by the only interior wall; concrete floors, mahogany panels, and zinc countertops constitute an uncomplicated palette.

ABOVE AND RIGHT: A series of outdoor terraces and patios connect the house to the outdoors and layered views over the Napa Valley.

WAGNER RESIDENCE

ARCHITECT WAGNER MCCANN STUDIO, BIRDSEYE BUILDING COMPANY
LOCATION NORTH FERRISBURGH, VERMONT

A collaboration between an architect and the owner, who is also a landscape architect and artist, resulted in this simple farm house, which is fully integrated with the landscape.

The approach to the house is along a straight drive that passes through meadows to a sculpture garden and a bosquet of honey locust before ending at the house. The sculpture garden contains large spheres of rusted metal that sit in contrast to the linear lines of the house and recall familiar rolled hay bales, repeating the patterns and rhythms of the rural New England landscape.

Influenced by the flat land and open sky, the house is a pared-down barn form, based on traditional Vermont styles and set into the meadow. An assembly of metal outbuildings—a sculpture studio and a chicken coop/painting studio—are connected to the main house by the landscape. The house is straightforward, combining simple, industrial agrarian materials conveyed though the rural vernacular architecture. The Wagner Residence design employs board-and-batten and metal siding, steel, glass, and concrete.

Inside, the floor plan is open and light. High, 11 foot ceilings and transoms over the windows enable views of the sky from any point in the house. The exterior materials—concrete, steel and glass—are carried inside. The floors are concrete with radiant heat. A simple, concrete-block fireplace defines the living area. The adjoining dining area is centered by a large table. In good weather, two glass garage doors roll up to create an open breezeway through the house and expand the public area outside.

In the kitchen area, industrial steel tables serve as counters, with steel tool cases beneath for drawer space. An enclosed pantry provides storage for small objects and clutter. The far edge of the dining area is defined by stacks of architectural shelving. Beyond are two bedrooms, including a master bedroom suite with maple flooring and radiant heat. An outdoor shower is located off the master bedroom.

A gravel terrace outside on the south end of the house enlarges on the west side to become a dining terrace. Beyond, the house is surrounded by meadows. A freestanding concrete wall, poured in place, defines the edge of the sculpture courtyard and expands the line of the house. Though new, the raw quality of the wall suggests an old foundation from a building that has long disappeared.

PHOTOGRAPHERS JIM WESTPHALEN, H. KEITH WAGNER

FLOOR PLAN

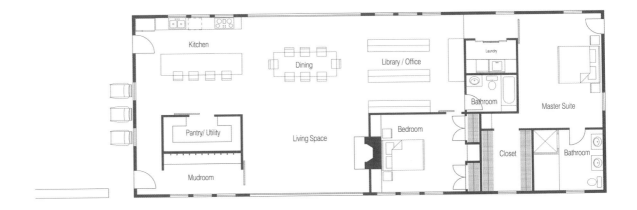

PREVIOUS PAGES: The architect collaborated with the owner, a landscape architect and artist, to create a house that is fully integrated with the landscape.

Kitchen

Dining

Library / Office

Laundry

Bathroom

Master Suite

Pantry/ Utility

Living Space

Bedroom

Closet

Bathroom

Mudroom

SITE PLAN

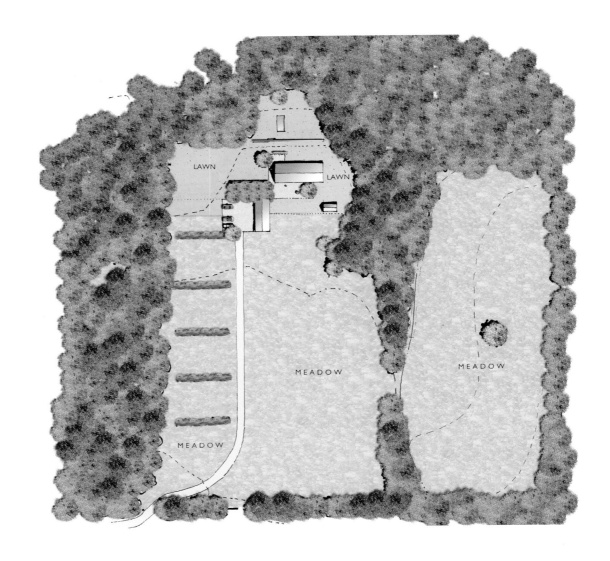

LAWN

LAWN

MEADOW

MEADOW

MEADOW

NORTH ELEVATION

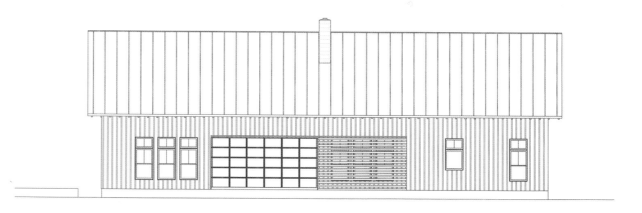

SOUTH ELEVATION

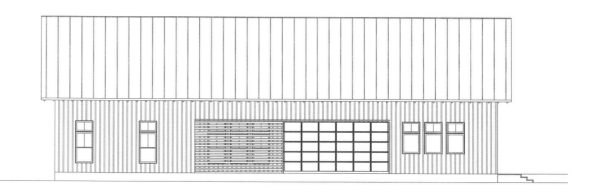

WEST ELEVATION

EAST ELEVATION

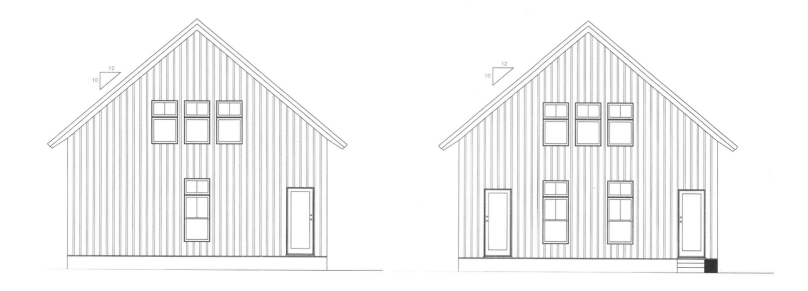

LEFT: The house is a pared-down barn form, based on traditional Vermont vernacular and set against the open sky and flat landscape. BELOW LEFT: Large spherical sculptures created by the owner evoke the rolled hay bales seen across the New England countryside. ABOVE: Connected to the main house by the landscape are two metal outbuildings, a sculpture studio and a chicken coop/painting studio. RIGHT: The edge of the sculpture courtyard is defined by a freestanding, raw concrete wall that suggests the foundation of a building that has long disappeared.

LEFT: The interior plan is open and light, made possible by high ceilings and transoms over the windows that permit a view of the sky from any point in the house. Interior materials are industrial agrarian——steel, glass, and concrete. A simple, concrete-block fireplace defines the living area. ABOVE: A breezeway is created through the house when the two garage doors are raised in good weather. Industrial steel tables serve as kitchen counters. Steel tool cases beneath provide drawer space. FOLLOWING PAGES: The house is minimalist and straightforward, drawing on industrial materials typically used for agrarian structures.

JONES FARMSTEAD

ARCHITECT SALMELA ARCHITECTURE AND DESIGN
LOCATION MINNESOTA

Built for a couple who retired early and moved to the countryside in southern Minnesota to pursue farming as a business, this new house was intended to function as a working farm as well as a comfortable home for the owners and a gathering place for grown children. To store field equipment, a barn was also needed.

The farm is surrounded by more than 100 acres of rolling grasslands, much of it preserved for future generations through a land trust. A portion of the land has been set aside to grow native grass seed for the agricultural market.

To take advantage of open views across the neighboring farms, the house is situated just below and north of the tallest hill. A looping drive enters the farmstead between the long garage to the north and the house to the south. While reflecting rural architectural structures, the house has a contemporary, relaxed quality without suburban fussiness.

The house is a Miesian plan with a 360-degree view. Kitchen, dining, and living areas extend in linear sequence ending in the rounded library at the north "silo" end of the house. The space includes a kitchen island, an enclosed staircase, and an open, stone-faced square hearth with a wood heater. A light reflection loft on the second floor hovers above the living space. The master bedroom has an exercise pool, workroom, and laundry. The barn is separate from the house, connected by a common roof to create a south facing court. Aside from space for machinery on the lower level, the barn also contains an office and guest space for family and friends.

The forms are familiar—silos, granaries, and outbuildings—and reflect a rural logic, in response to the southern Minnesota landscape. Materials are common and straightforward—brick, metal seamed roofing, recycled fir, and cypress—all applied in the vernacular way.

PHOTOGRAPHER PETER BASTIANELLI KERZE

SITE PLAN/FLOOR PLAN

PREVIOUS PAGES AND BELOW: Rolling grassland, much of it in preservation for future generations through a land trust, surrounds this working farm in southern Minnesota. To take advantage of these open views, the house is placed just below and north of the tallest hill.

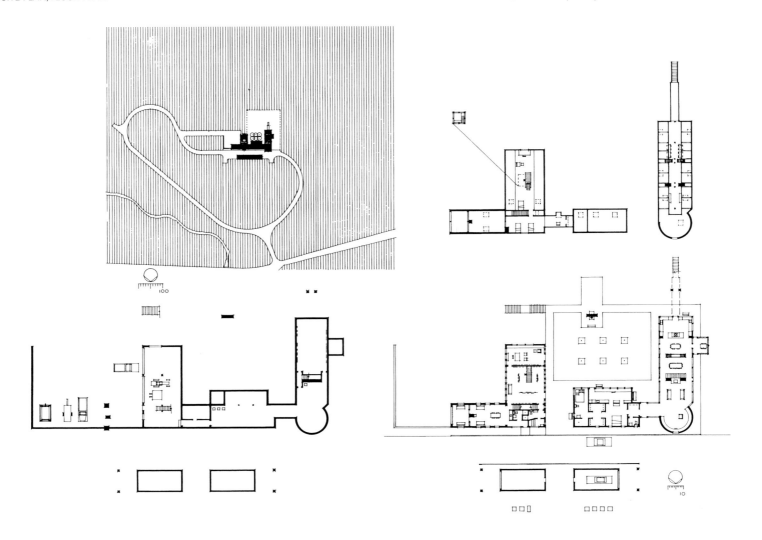

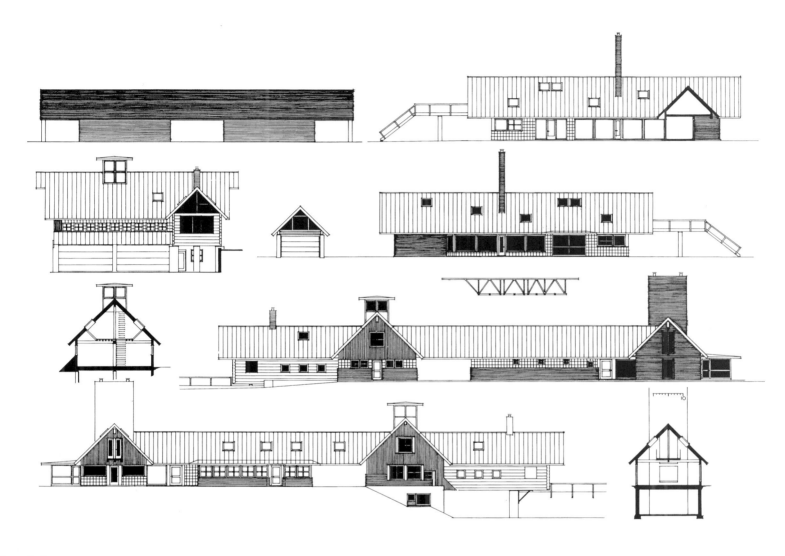

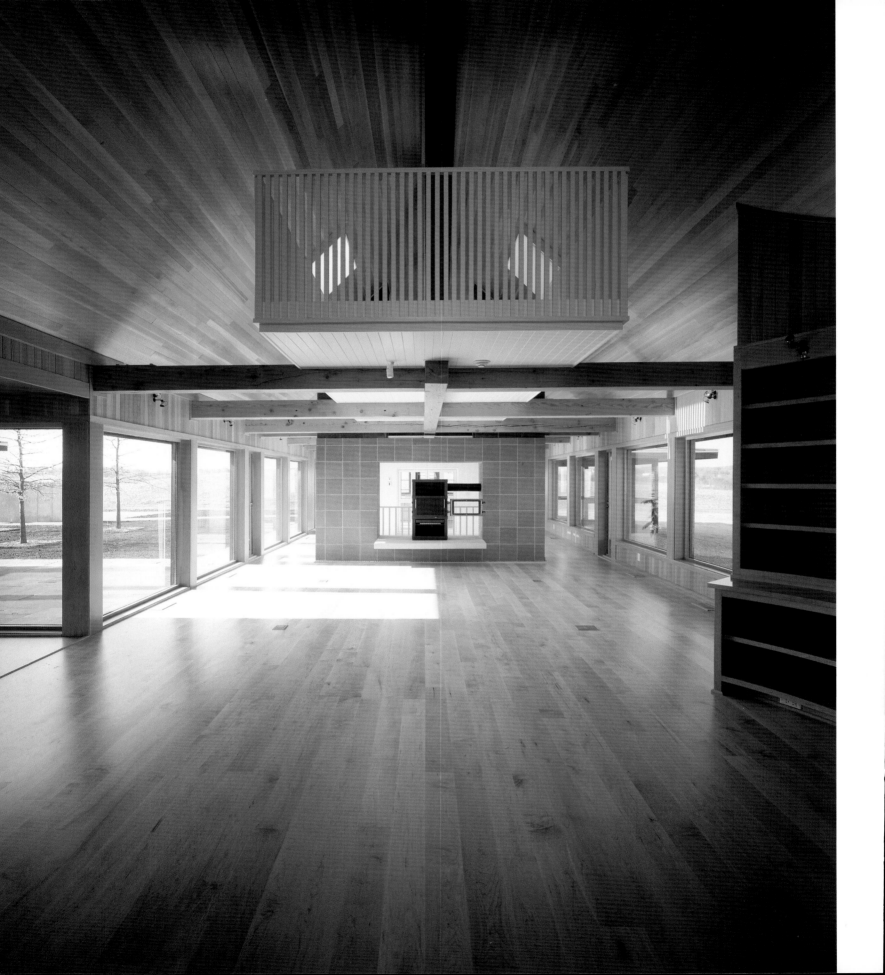

LEFT AND ABOVE: The house is a Miesian plan with kitchen, dining, and living areas extending in linear sequence. Spaces are defined by the kitchen island, an enclosed staircase, and an open, stone-faced square fireplace with a wood heater.

ABOVE: A rounded library is placed in the north "silo" end of the house.

ABOVE LEFT: The master bedroom with an attached workroom and laundry.
ABOVE: The light reflection loft floats above the living space below.

ABOVE: Separate from the house, the barn is connected by a common roof to create a south-facing court. The barn has an office space and bedrooms for visiting family and friends. Machinery is stored below on a lower level. RIGHT: A guest bedroom in the barn is paneled in wood. FOLLOWING PAGES: Rural forms——silos, granaries, and outbuildings ——harmonize with the southern Minnesota landscape.

LITTLE BIG HOUSE

ARCHITECT SHIPLEY ARCHITECTS
LOCATION EULOGY, TEXAS

This house pays homage to local barns found in the rolling Texas Hill Country outside Dallas. Designed as a small house, only 1,600 square feet, that could function like a much larger one, it is a perfect country retreat for a Dallas couple, their children and grandchildren. Flexible, open spaces encourage circulation, but also offer a measure of privacy when needed. It is a program that works, since family reunions here sometimes draw as many as 100 guests.

The house blends naturally into the surrounding landscape—rough country dotted with cedar and oak, interspersed with grassland. This was a working cattle ranch until the early twentieth century, and the stone ruins of the old farm house still remain on the property.

Similar to agricultural buildings of the 19th century, the house is built up from a central structure with sheds flanking either side. The central volume contains the open public spaces, including the living and dining areas.

The east shed is a double-height, screened porch with an upper deck. The screened porch extends the floor space of the living room out into the landscape.

The west shed contains the kitchen and three bedrooms, all oriented to a central, two-story space. On the first floor are the master bedroom and bath, privately placed off the kitchen. Above, the two second-floor bedrooms open loft-like through French doors to the central area.

The sheds on either side of the central structure are connected at the second-floor level with a bridge across the living room to the upper deck, which resembles a pier stretching out. From the upper deck, which also can serve as a sleeping loft for children, there are expansive views of the distant landscape.

Outside, the deep roofline—supported by two beams—projects out over a stone patio, providing a shaded retreat on the south side of the house.

The interior detailing is clean and tightly controlled. Local Granbury stone is used as veneer on the interior and exterior. Cedar clapboard siding covers the interior walls of the central space.

PHOTOGRAPHER JAMES F. WILSON, DEBORA HUNTER

SECOND FLOOR PLAN

FIRST FLOOR PLAN

1. FRONT PORCH
2. DINING
3. LIVING
4. SCREENED PORCH
5. KITCHEN
6. BEDROOM
7. STONE PORCH
8. BRIDGE
9. DECK

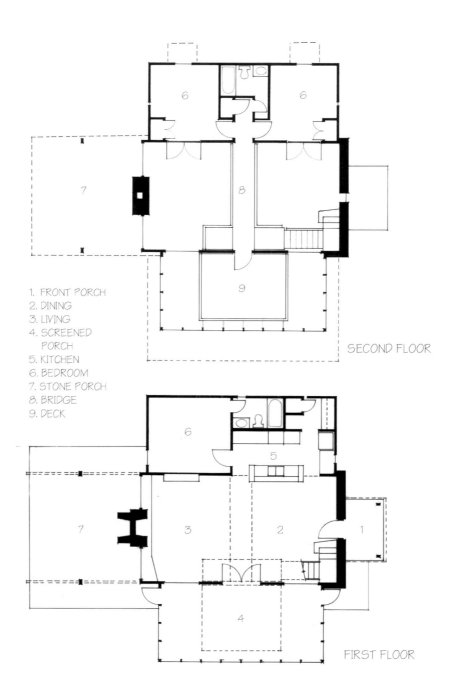

SECOND FLOOR

FIRST FLOOR

LEFT: Inside, the plan is flexible and open, but also provides privacy for a Dallas couple and their grown family. The program works well, since family reunions here sometimes draw as many as 100 guests. ABOVE: Public spaces, including the living and dining areas, are contained in the central, stone-veneered volume of the house. Cedar clapboard siding covers the interior walls.

ABOVE: A bridge across the living room to the upper deck connects the two sheds on either side of the central structure. RIGHT: The interior detailing is clean and tightly controlled. Local Granbury stone is used as veneer on the interior and exterior. FAR RIGHT: Doors from the two second-floor bedrooms open to the central space.

LEFT: A stone patio is shaded by a broad roofline supported by rough beams. RIGHT: The east shed is a screened porch that extends the living room out into the landscape. An upper deck projects outward over the first floor.

CHAUVIN FARM HOUSE

ARCHITECT HOLLY AND SMITH ARCHITECTS
LOCATION LOUISIANA

The rural Louisiana setting inspired the design for this house, once part of a farm owned by the parents of the clients—a local artist and his wife—the fields now grow flowers for a fresh-cut flower market. The goal was to design a farm house that reflected the Louisiana regional vernacular, which would also be well suited to the harsh, humid climate. At the same time, the young couple wanted the new house to be a fresh, modern environment. Also important, the house needed to co-exist with a number of centuries old live oak trees and not damage their delicate root structure.

In response to the hot, humid climate of south Louisiana, the linear house form is oriented on an east-west axis to minimize solar gain. Expansive windows, set back under veranda-type porches, line the north and south façades. Awning louvers and deep overhangs provide shading for other openings. To obstruct the sun's harsh low rays from the east and west, all openings on the narrow east and west faces are kept to a minimum.

The house is segmented into three distinct pods: the central main house pod with the living room, dining room, kitchen, and second floor loft studio; the master suite pod; and the guest suite/garage pod. The pods are each essentially separate buildings, connected by transparent bridges that serve as transition spaces between changes in the design program. The fireplace is a freestanding tower within the main space and is located along the east-west building axis at the entry to the master suite. The tower serves to mark the living-space focal point, while assisting in providing privacy to the master suite. The main house pod, although a compact floor plan, spatially references a barn-like interior. This is accomplished by the open second floor loft supported by heavy timber framework extending through the space. The stair structure, built from glue-laminated beams, has open risers reminiscent of a ladder up to the loft studio.

PHOTOGRAPHER MARC LAMKIN

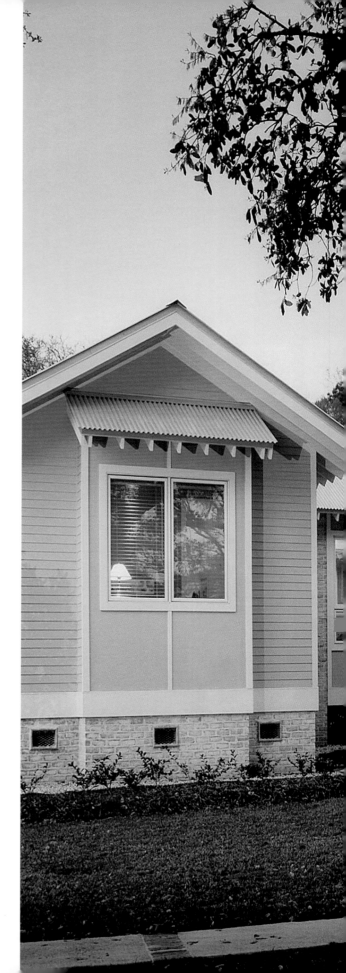

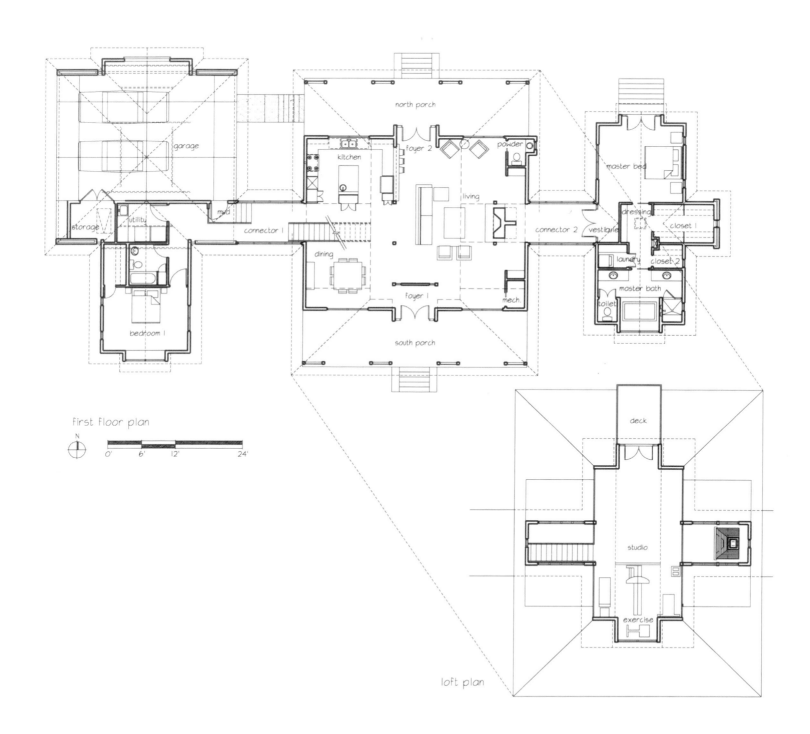

PREVIOUS PAGES: The Louisiana countryside inspired the design for this house, a "farm house" that reflected the regional vernacular, suitable for the harsh humid climate.

first floor plan

N

0'   6'   12'   24'

loft plan

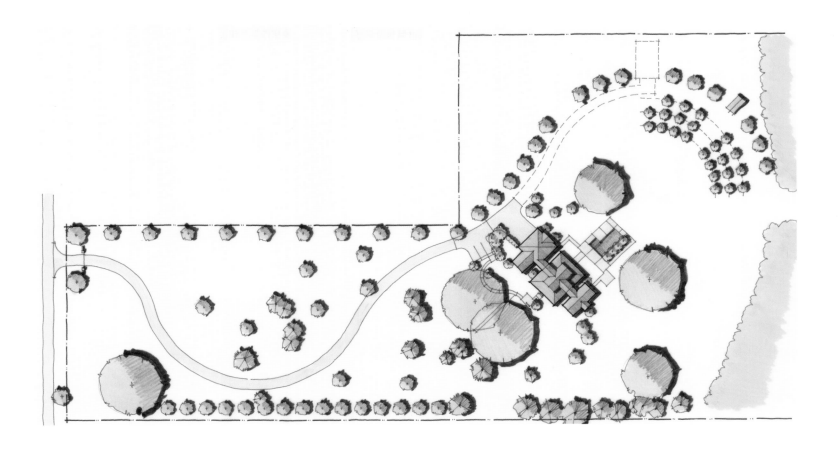

south elevation

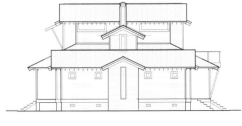

west elevation

north elevation

0' 6' 12'   24'

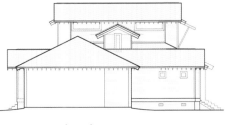

east elevation

ABOVE: Expansive windows, set back under veranda-type porches, line the north and south façades. Awning louvers and deep overhangs provide shading for other openings.

BELOW: To limit the sun's harsh low rays from the east and west, all openings on the narrow east and west faces are kept to a minimum.

ABOVE: The living room area in the main house pod features an open, compact floor plan, and spatially references a barn-like interior. This is reinforced by the open second floor loft supported by heavy timber framework extending through the space. LEFT: The dining area, along with the kitchen and the living area, forms the central main house pod.

ABOVE: The fireplace is a freestanding tower within the main space that serves to mark the living-space focal point while providing privacy to the master suite. RIGHT: The kitchen opens to the living room. FOLLOWING PAGES: The house is segmented into three distinct pods, essentially separate buildings connected by transparent bridges that serve as transition spaces between changes in the design program.

NAPA FARM HOUSE

ARCHITECTS OSBORN DESIGN GROUP, MAD ARCHITECTURE
LOCATION NAPA, CALIFORNIA

Through a radical renovation, a 1980s contractor spec house in the Napa Valley was transformed into a spacious, contemporary farm house. The original house was a two-story clapboard box with a warren of tiny rooms and low ceilings inside. While the owners loved the location, vineyards, and views across open fields, they wanted fewer, more open spaces.

The new additions harmonize with the original form of the house, but add contrast. A new cedar breezeway with a flat metal roof was attached, creating consistency with the exisiting roof. Breaking from the clapboard box, the south side has a silo sheathed in metal and projected volumes sided with cement fiber panels and exposed fasteners. The existing wraparound porch was re-roofed, and new railings were added.

To open up the house inside on the ground floor, solid shear walls were removed and replaced with steell-beams and pipe columns. Part of the second floor was removed to create a two-story entry, stairs and gallery space thus lending all adjacent spaces a greater sense of height. This gallery area displays the owner's art collection. The open staircase, made of steel, cables, and thick cherry treads, creates a visual center for the downstairs level and the open living-area, dining-area, and kitchen. A library/music studio is located behind the staircase.

On the second level, a master suite was created. The master bath was the only floor area added to the original house; on the exterior, it projects over the deck, creating a covered outdoor space on the south side of the dining room. It provides a sheltered eating area with a view of the garden. The silo serves as a reading room off the master suite and acts as a cooling tower capturing the morning light from the north side of the house.

The material palette is rural and contemporary, including aluminum windows, steel columns, oak floors, cherry cabinets and details, cedar skip sheathing, cedar cabinets, Beau Marnier limestone, exterior wood siding, cement fiber panels, plywood and batten, corrugated metal, and standing seam roofing.

PHOTOGRAPHER TIM MALONEY

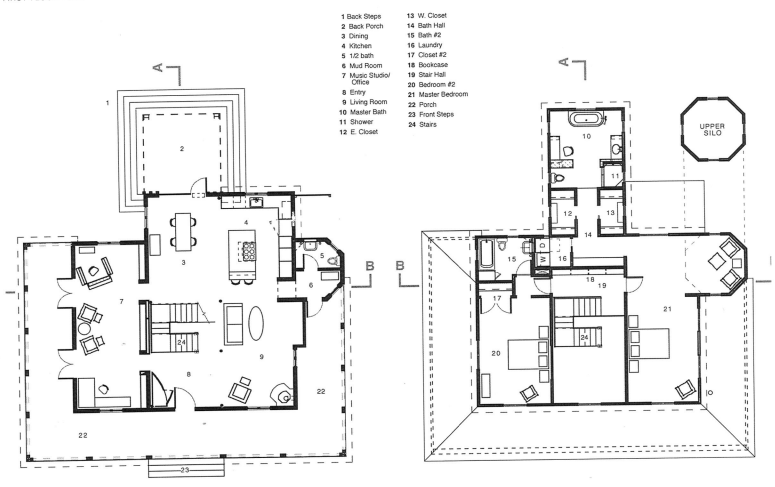

PREVIOUS PAGES: A radical renovation transformed this 1980s contractor spec house in the Napa Valley into a spacious, contemporary farm house. The original house was a two-story clapboard box with a warren of tiny rooms and low ceilings inside.

BELOW: Seen from the rear, new additions harmonize and add contrast to the original form.

FIRST FLOOR PLAN

SECOND FLOOR PLAN

1 Back Steps
2 Back Porch
3 Dining
4 Kitchen
5 1/2 bath
6 Mud Room
7 Music Studio/
  Office
8 Entry
9 Living Room
10 Master Bath
11 Shower
12 E. Closet

13 W. Closet
14 Bath Hall
15 Bath #2
16 Laundry
17 Closet #2
18 Bookcase
19 Stair Hall
20 Bedroom #2
21 Master Bedroom
22 Porch
23 Front Steps
24 Stairs

EAST ELEVATION

SOUTH ELEVATION

WEST ELEVATION

NORTH ELEVATION

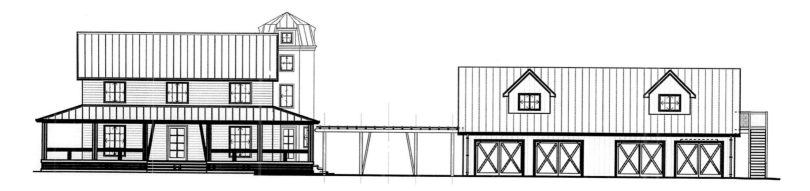

LEFT TOP: Breaking from the clapboard box, the south side has a silo sheathed in metal and projected volumes sided with cement fiber panels and exposed fasteners. Inside, the silo serves as a reading room off the master suite and acts as a cooling tower, capturing the morning light from the north side of the house. LEFT: A new cedar breezeway with a flat metal roof connects the house to the garage, which has a studio guest apartment above the parking and storage area. ABOVE: The master bath projects outside, over the deck, creating a covered outdoor space on the south side of the dining room, providing a sheltered eating area with a view of the garden.

LEFT: Part of the second floor was removed to create a two-story entry, stair, and gallery space thus lending all adjacent spaces a greater sense of height. This gallery area displays the owner's art collection.
RIGHT: The open staircase, made of steel, cables, and thick cherry treads, creates a visual center for the downstairs level and the open living-area, dining-area, and kitchen.

ABOVE: A library/music studio is located behind the staircase. RIGHT
TOP: The only floor area added to the original house, the master bath
projects outside over the deck, creating a covered outdoor space.
RIGHT: The kitchen has simple, recessed panel cabinets. The island,
raised on legs, reinforces the open feeling.

DOG TROT HOUSE

ARCHITECT WAGGONNER & BALL ARCHITECTS
LOCATION POPLARVILLE, MISSISSIPPI

A weekend retreat for a New Orleans couple, this small house of less than 1,000 square feet is sited in the rural hills of southern Mississippi overlooking a small pond. Set in a context of small farms, scrubland, and intermittent pine forest, the house draws its form and materiality from the simple vernacular prototypes seen in the neighboring fields: small barns, chicken coops, tin sheds, and "enhanced" mobile homes.

The dog trot prototype, typical in the rural South, was the plan generator, making the house a frame or gateway for the pond and landscape beyond. This open space, which serves as a sheltered and informal dining porch, provides a cool, breezy place to sit on hot days.

The open porch divides and defines the functions of the structure, which comprises four cells: a storage/workroom, the dining porch, a living space, and a screened porch. The storage bay can be accessed at grade level for maintenance equipment. The living space is a double height volume with a sleeping loft above closets and a bathroom. The adjoining screened porch is perched on the crest of an incline and overlooks a swampy corner of the pond.

The house is of wood-frame construction on an unpainted concrete block base. Stained board-and-batten siding is interlaced with horizontal weatherboard siding. A single-slope standing seam metal roof is a diagonal counterpoint to a freestanding masonry chimney serving an outdoor fireplace. Broad steps and a raised concrete deck extend the center dog trot space into the landscape.

PHOTOGRAPHER WAGGONER & BALL, AND KERRI MCCAFFETY

FLOOR PLAN

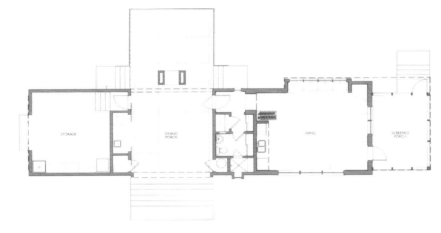

SECTION

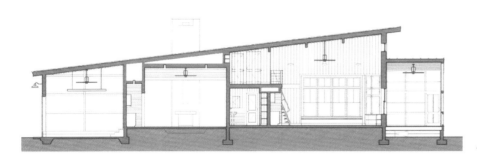

PREVIOUS PAGES AND BELOW: The plan for this house draws from the dog trot prototype, typical in the rural South. The open dog trot provides a sheltered and informal dining porch and a shaded refuge on hot days. Broad steps and a raised concrete deck extend the center dog trot space into the landscape. RIGHT: The surrounding landscape is defined by small farms, scrubland, and pine forest. Simple vernacular prototypes from the area—small barns, chicken coops, tin sheds, and "enhanced" mobile homes—suggested the design and materials for this house.

NORTH ELEVATION

EAST ELEVATION

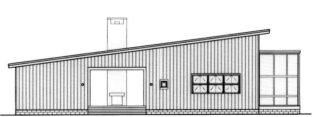

WEST ELEVATION

ABOVE LEFT: The house forms a frame or gateway for the pond and landscape beyond. ABOVE: Stained board-and-batten siding is used on the exterior, interlaced with horizontal weatherboard siding. The house is of wood-frame construction on an unpainted concrete-block base. RIGHT: The living space is a double-height volume with a sleeping loft above closets and a bathroom. Simple pine boards are used to face the interior walls.

ABOVE: Window seat RIGHT: One of four cells that form the structure, the adjoining screened porch overlooks a swampy corner of the pond. FOLLOWING PAGES: Located in the rural hills of southern Mississippi, this uncomplicated weekend home provides a quiet retreat for a New Orleans couple.

COASTAL RETREAT

ARCHITECT AIDLIN DARLING DESIGN
LOCATION NORTHERN CALIFORNIA

The landscape of the Northern California coast is marked by patterns of dense forest and open clearing, which create a sequence of alternating sun and shade. This rhythm punctuates the approach to this woodland site and informs the careful placement of three structures into a glen of existing trees. This house, garage, and artist's studio are nestled into intimate clearings with distant ocean views to the west. The northeastern corner is dug slightly into the hillside, while the southwestern edge elevates toward the view. This gesture locks the house into the landscape and gives it a sense of permanence.

Vernacular forms of local Northern Californian agricultural-industrial buildings, designed for utility and survival, inspired the construction of the house. Natural materials were selected for their warmth, their direct connection to the natural world, and their ability to weather gracefully in a coastal environment. Battered board-form concrete walls create a solid foundation for a skin of redwood siding and recycled-redwood doors and windows. The copper roof has deep overhangs, protecting the wood skin and sheltering indoor/outdoor transitions. Interior finishes are primarily wood and plaster, and cabinetry is articulated as furniture to further domesticate each room.

The house is organized around a central living room with an anchoring concrete hearth. Arranged in the form of an "H," other spaces connect directly to this central great room, with private bedrooms to one side and an open kitchen and dining room to the other. Each space has a direct connection to the exterior, with the outdoor spaces maintaining equal significance to the life of the house as the interior.

It is with great respect for this virgin land that these three structures were delicately placed. Over time, this coastal retreat will age gracefully and blend with its environment.

PHOTOGRAPHER JOHN SUTTON, CESAR RUBIO

NORTH ELEVATION

FLOOR PLAN

PREVIOUS PAGES: This Northern California house was inspired by vernacular forms of local agricultural-industrial buildings that were designed for utility and endurance. The house, as well as an artist's studio and garage, are nestled into clearings. To the west, there are distant views of the ocean. BELOW RIGHT: Redwood, which weathers gracefully in the coastal environment, was selected for the warmth it imparts and the connection to the surrounding forest. Redwood siding and recycled-redwood doors and windows were used.

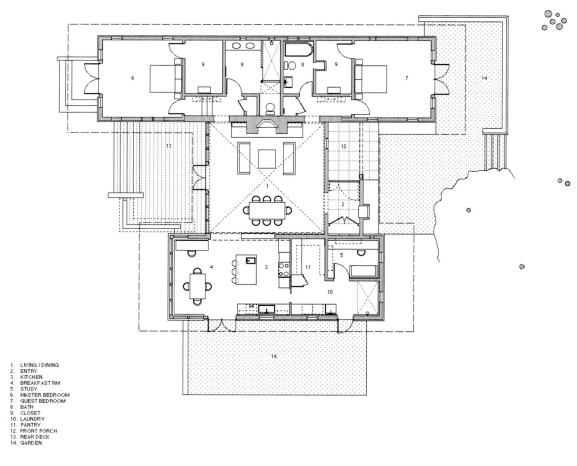

1. LIVING / DINING
2. ENTRY
3. KITCHEN
4. BREAKFAST RM
5. STUDY
6. MASTER BEDROOM
7. GUEST BEDROOM
8. BATH
9. CLOSET
10. LAUNDRY
11. PANTRY
12. FRONT PORCH
13. REAR DECK
14. GARDEN

ELEVATIONS

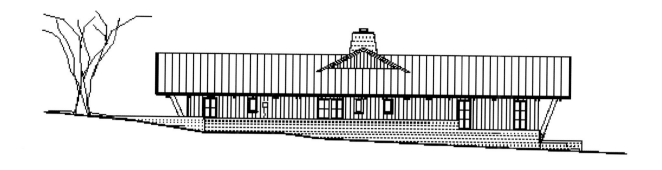

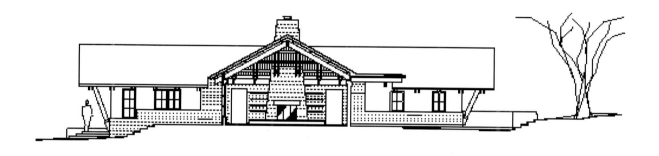

SITE PLAN

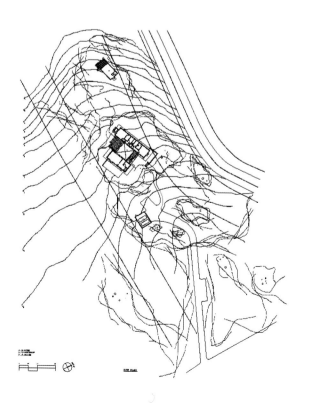

LEFT AND BELOW: Deep overhangs shelter indoor/outdoor transitions. Each indoor space connects to the exterior; the outdoor spaces are as significant to the life of the house as the interior ones. Batten board-form concrete walls create a solid foundation.

ABOVE AND RIGHT: The house is arranged in the form of an "H" organized around a central living room. A tapered concrete hearth anchors this central great room. Interior finishes are primarily wood and plaster. ABOVE RIGHT AND FAR RIGHT: An open kitchen and dining room connect directly to the central great room. Cabinetry is articulated as furniture in each room.

ABOVE AND RIGHT: An artist's studio was also built in the clearing.
FOLLOWING PAGES: The three structures were placed into the landscape
with sensitivity and respect, and over time this coastal retreat will age
gracefully and blend with its surroundings.

HOLMES FARMSTEAD

ARCHITECT SALMELA ARCHITECTURE AND DESIGN
LOCATION MINNESOTA

This white farm house sits on a gently flowing river in northern Minnesota surrounded by lush meadows and fields. Designed as a small, functional home for a couple with grown children, the house measures only 1,820 square feet The plan features a master bedroom on the main level, and a private guest cottage, which accommodates visiting children and grandchildren.

While the simple rural forms and materials, along with the restrained palette recall the modest farm houses of Minnesota's countryside, the design is clearly modern. The house uses 18-foot-wide modules, in straight and staggered positions, wrapping around an entry court. The modules are attached by slightly curved roofed corridors.

On the exterior, the combination of board-and-batten and clapboard siding provides textural interest. The irregular arrangement of windows is contemporary in feeling. Several outdoor spaces provide options to sit and enjoy the pastoral setting, and a deck located off the living room has a curved-roof pergola that references the curved ceilings inside.

A picket fence encloses a barnyard, leading to an entryway with a curved roof that suggests a separate rural outbuilding. Inside, the kitchen and dining area, living room, and master bedroom are staggered in sequence, though spatially connected. Windows flood the rooms with natural light, and a large corner window in the living room creates the feeling of an enclosed porch. Curved pine ceilings add warmth, and minimal interior detailing reinforces the casual rural statement. Outbuildings include a cabinetmaking shop, an equipment garage, and a chicken coop.

PHOTOGRAPHER   PETER BASTIANELLI KERZE

PREVIOUS PAGES: Lush meadows and a gently flowing river provide the setting for this white farm house in northern Minnesota. The house uses 18-foot wide modules in straight and staggered positions. The simple, rural forms recall the modest farm houses of Minnesota's countryside, but the design is clearly modern. BELOW: Outdoor spaces provide an opportunity to enjoy the surrounding meadows and fields. The deck located off the living room has a curved-roof pergola that references the curved ceilings inside.

SITE PLAN/FLOOR PLAN

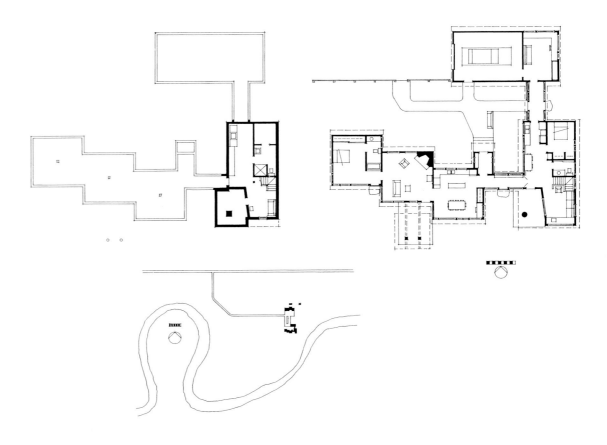

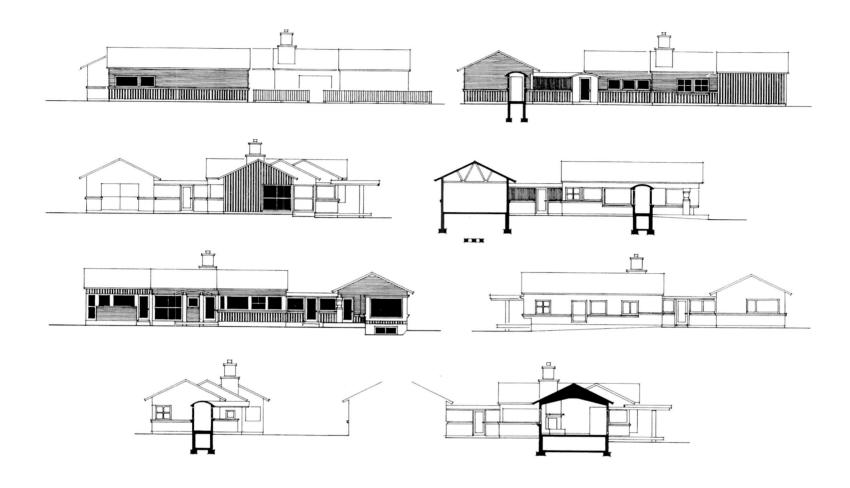

LEFT: The kitchen and dining area, living room, and master bedroom are staggered in sequence. Curved pine ceilings inside add warmth. Minimal interior detailing reinforces the casual rural statement. A large corner window in the living room creates the feeling of an enclosed porch. FOLLOWING PAGES: An enclosed entry court suggests a farmyard with a picket fence.

FREEMAN FARM HOUSE

ARCHITECT SALA ARCHITECTS
LOCATION RIVER FALLS, WISCONSIN

A pastoral meadow landscape inspired this low-cost house, built on the owner's 160-acre farm in rural Wisconsin. The clients and the architects sought to design an energy-efficient house that was modest in scope, and would reflect the aesthetic of older midwestern agrarian buildings. The house also had to interact with an existing barn and garage structure in an open, cultivated field.

To meet a budget, relatively inexpensive materials were adapted and creative design decisions were made, which lowered construction costs. The result is a building of its place that expresses the rural Wisconsin vernacular in a simple, direct, and cost-conscious way.

The nearly 2,000 square-foot house features an open, contemporary floor plan with varied ceiling heights and few interior walls, a decision that supported the owner's interest in functional spaces that would be used every day, but also helped with the budget. Only four rooms—an office, two bathrooms, and the utility room—are enclosed by walls and doors. The upstairs bedroom is a loft. No basement was built, which also lowered construction costs.

Simple, honest materials and details were employed, reminiscent of those found on old agricultural buildings in Wisconsin. Corrugated galvanized siding used outside lends harmony to exterior, but is also low maintenance and relatively inexpensive. Inside, the siding was also used in both bathrooms to surround the baths. Concrete floors were poured on the first level and an in-floor radiant heating system conveys heat upward to warm the second floor. The concrete also helps keep the house cool in summer. Some concrete block was left exposed in the walls of the downstairs bathroom and laundry room, saving money on finishing costs. Built-in birch cabinetry and shelving saves space throughout the house.

PHOTOGRAPHER GEORGE HEINRICH

SECOND FLOOR PLAN

FIRST FLOOR PLAN

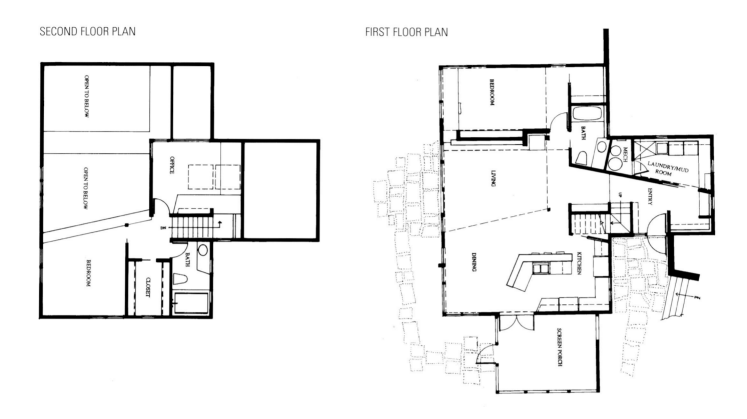

OPEN TO BELOW

OPEN TO BELOW

OFFICE

DN

BEDROOM

BATH

CLOSET

BEDROOM

BATH

LIVING

MECH

LAUNDRY/MUD ROOM

UP

ENTRY

DINING

KITCHEN

DN

SCREEN PORCH

EAST ELEVATION

WEST ELEVATION

NORTH ELEVATION

SOUTH ELEVATION

LEFT AND ABOVE: The interior features an open, contemporary floor plan with varied ceiling heights and few interior walls. Poured-concrete floors with radiant heating were used on the first floor, for both low maintenance and cost.

ABOVE: A loft upstairs serves as a bedroom. Simple materials and
construction details were used throughout the house. RIGHT: Corrugated
galvanized siding was used in both bathrooms to surround the baths.
FOLLOWING PAGES: Rural forms and details are expressed in a fully
contemporary manner.

WILD HAIR

ARCHITECT MELL LAWRENCE ARCHITECTS
LOCATION DRIFTWOOD, TEXAS

The traditional barns and rural vernacular of the Texas countryside were the starting point for this country home outside of Austin. What appears at first glance to be a red barn tucked away in a rural subdivision is actually a very up-to-date house that incorporates many sustainable and energy-efficient features.

Despite the simple form, each of the building's four sides is unique, responding to the site and the room function within. The roofline on the south side is dramatically extended to accommodate a large screened porch, which serves as an outdoor living room and adds unexpected visual drama to the essentially symmetrical volume. At night, the polycarbonate roof glows like a lantern.

In a play off the house's rural roots, unique and sometimes whimsical design elements are found throughout. Materials were carefully selected for durability and aesthetics, as well as sustainability, and then applied creatively. Inside, the house is simple, clean, and modern. Large, commercial-grade windows were carefully placed to capture both views and breezes, bringing the outdoors in, and creating a continuously changing ambience. Exterior and interior doors recall the sliding doors typically found in barns and agricultural outbuildings. Concrete floors are easy to maintain and stay cool in the summer.

The open plan of the living areas promotes the flow and togetherness sought by the owners and makes the home—just over 2,000 square feet—seem much larger. Upstairs, the bedrooms and bath are located off a central hallway and were deliberately kept on the small side to encourage family members to enjoy the public spaces.

The house is fully wired for Internet access and features a wireless security system, yet it operates solely on rainwater collected in a 10,000 gallon tank located on the property. To take advantage of the prevailing breezes, the house is positioned on the east-west axis. The house is made of structural insulated panels that save energy, and incorporaes low maintenance materials like Hardiplank and concrete for the floors on the first level. A metal roof helps reflect the Texas heat.

PHOTOGRAPHER PAUL HESTER

SECOND FLOOR PLAN

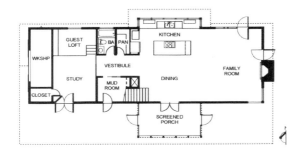

SITE PLAN

LEFT: The interior of the house features an open plan with simple, clean details and finishes. Materials such as concrete and stone were selected for durability and aesthetics. BELOW: The open plan encourages family members to use the public spaces and makes the home——just over 2,000 square feet——seem much larger.

ABOVE: Reflecting the house's rural roots, whimsical references to farm buildings are used both inside and out. Interior doors recall the sliding doors typically found in barns and agricultural outbuildings. RIGHT: The kitchen is fully open to the dining and living areas. FOLLOWING PAGES: Wild Hair nestled among the trees

SCRABBLETOWN HOUSE

ARCHITECT DURKEE, BROWN, VIVEIROS & WERENFELS
LOCATION NORTH KINGSTON, RHODE ISLAND

The village of Scrabbletown in North Kingston, Rhode Island, is the setting for this 2,000 square-foot farm house. So called because early residents had to "scrabble" to make a living from the rocky farmland, Scrabbletown today still contains remnants of an earlier era despite the encroachment of suburban development. Mature trees, old fence posts, and ancient stone walls remain and speak to the area's humbler, rural origins.

In this new, single-family house, elements of barns and other utilitarian rural structures are combined with modern features to create a hybrid building with a separate garage and workshop. Modest forms and materials typically associated with rural buildings are carefully detailed for simple construction.

The house and garage/workshop are organized around a central garden that links the buildings to the outdoors. The buildings frame views of the landscape, while the garden acts as negative space and permits vistas the full length of the site.

The entryway to the house—clad in galvanized corrugated steel—suggests the end of a barn or a silo and connects to the larger structure by a short hall. This main section features an open plan downstairs with connected living and dining areas. Cabinetry partitions serve as partial walls and provide a sense of enclosure for the kitchen. A deep overhang created by the second floor shelters an outdoor patio by the kitchen garden, accessed through French doors from the dining area. Upstairs is a master bedroom and bath and two other bedrooms.

To the north of the house, beyond an old farm wall, is a vegetable garden and a chicken coop—also designed by the architect—with resident Rhode Island Reds.

PHOTOGRAPHER GLENN TURNER

SECOND FLOOR PLAN

Study/Bedroom

Bedroom   Bath

Master Bedroom

Bath

Workshop

PREVIOUS PAGES: This 2,000 square-foot house in Scrabbletown reflects the barns and other utilitarian rural buildings found in coastal New England. The house, however, is fully modern.

FIRST FLOOR PLAN

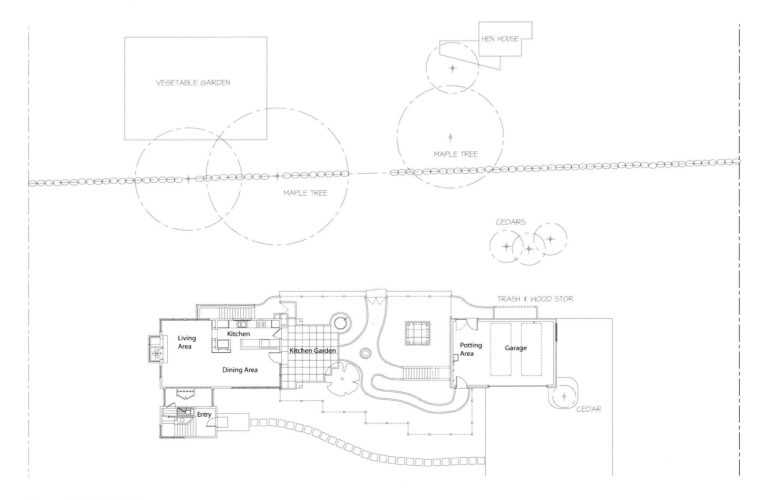

HEN HOUSE

VEGETABLE GARDEN

MAPLE TREE

MAPLE TREE

CEDARS

TRASH & WOOD STOR

Living Area

Kitchen

Kitchen Garden

Potting Area   Garage

Dining Area

Entry

CEDAR

NORTH ELEVATION

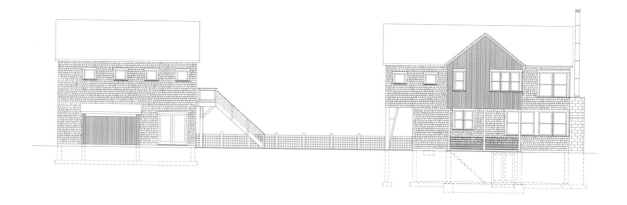

SOUTH ELEVATION

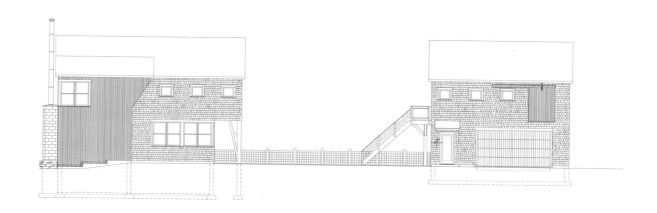

CONCEPT SKETCHES

ABOVE: The house and separate garage with workshop are organized around a central garden. The two buildings frame views of the landscape. LEFT: Forms and materials reminiscent of those associated with rural buildings have been adapted here. Corrugated steel and cedar shingles are used on the exterior.

ABOVE: An outdoor patio is tucked beneath a deep overhang created by the second floor and overlooks the kitchen garden. RIGHT: The central garden creates a connection to the outdoors and visually links the house with the garage and workshop.

ABOVE AND RIGHT: An open plan downstairs connects the living-areas and dining-areas, brightly lit by natural light. The kitchen is defined by partial cabinetry walls.

BUCKS COUNTY HOME

ARCHITECT DONALD BILLINKOFF ARCHITECTS
LOCATION TINICUM TOWNSHIP, PENNSYLVANIA

This Bucks County home, built by an expatriate Manhattan family is actually a collection of connected, small buildings that incorporates an original pre-Revolutionary stone farm house. The new, contemporary structures link to the old farm house and employ rural architectural forms and exterior materials that evoke the simple Quaker farm buildings found in this historic county which lies along the Delaware River.

Over the years, the original stone farm house had fallen into disrepair. In addition, the old building—with small rooms and low ceilings—was unsuited to a family with three children and weekend guests. The decision was made to renovate the farm house to serve as a private space, containing the master bedroom, an adjacent study, and three children's rooms, new bathrooms in a tower addition.

To provide space for public areas, a new main house was built and connected to the stone farm house by a 35-foot-long library corridor lined with windows that look into a courtyard and the yard beyond. The heart of the new building is a lofty great room with a massive, freestanding stone fireplace in the center, open on two sides. An airy, state-of-the-art stainless steel kitchen sits at one end, with an adjoining dining-area; opposite, separated by the fireplace, is the living area. Overlooking this space from the second floor is a loft with a glass-enclosed family room. Interior details, including exposed beam lintels, unpainted wood trim and fieldstone, reinforce the farm house references.

Built with summer living in mind, a 1,500 square-foot screened porch projects over the wildflower meadow that surrounds the buildings. Large enough for family dinners, the porch also houses a gas grill for year-round grilling. The garage is a separate structure with a guest apartment above.

PHOTOGRAPHER BARRY HALKIN

SECOND FLOOR PLAN

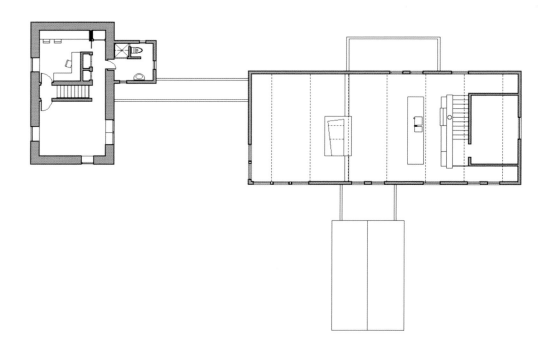

FIRST FLOOR PLAN

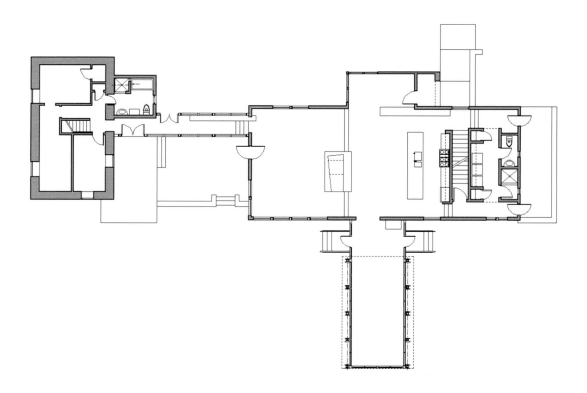

NORTHEAST ELEVATION

NORTHWEST ELEVATION

SOUTHWEST ELEVATION

ABOVE AND RIGHT: The house is actually a collection of connected, small buildings that incorporates an original pre-Revolutionary stone farm house. The decision was made to renovate the farm house to serve as a private space, containing the master bedroom, an adjacent study, and three children's rooms. New bathrooms were accommodated in a tower addition.

ABOVE: The new entry vestibule opens into the heart of the new building, a lofty great room with a massive, freestanding stone fireplace in the center, open on two sides. RIGHT: The living room is separated from the dining area and kitchen by a fieldstone fireplace.

ABOVE: An airy, state-of-the-art stainless steel kitchen sits at one end with an adjoining dining area; opposite, separated by the fireplace, is the living area. RIGHT: The original stone farmhouse serves as private space and contains the master bedroom and an adjacent study, as well as three children's bedrooms.

ABOVE: The screened porch projects out over the wildflower meadow that surrounds the buildings. LEFT: Built with summer living in mind, the 1,500 square-foot screened porch is large enough for family dinners.

RAPPAHANNOCK HOUSE

ARCHITECT MCINTURFF ARCHITECTS
LOCATION RAPPAHANNOCK COUNTY, VIRGINIA

With comanding views across acres of meadows to the distant Blue Ridge, this weekend house in rural Rappahannock County, Virginia, takes its inspiration from farm buildings and their assemblages, abstractly recalling local, rural building traditions through color, form, and organization.

The linear form of the house gives each major room a view of the mountains in the distance. Color is used inside and out to articulate the length of the building as three ochre pavilions with barn-red connectors. Gray-green, shed-roofed volumes form wings, defining a parking court on the approach side and a terrace on the view side. Locally familiar materials, such as Galvalume roofs and concrete-block fireplaces, further reinforce the vernacular.

Since the house was envisioned as a generous second home for weekend entertaining and extended family, the public rooms are spacious and open. The first pavilion contains a living room and music room. The dining-area and kitchen constitute the second or middle pavilion, and the third pavilion is a screened porch. The master bedroom and guest bedrooms are on the second floor.

PHOTOGRAPHER JULIA HEINE

THIRD FLOOR PLAN

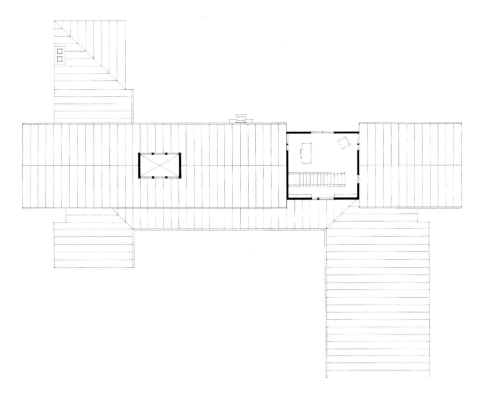

SECOND FLOOR PLAN

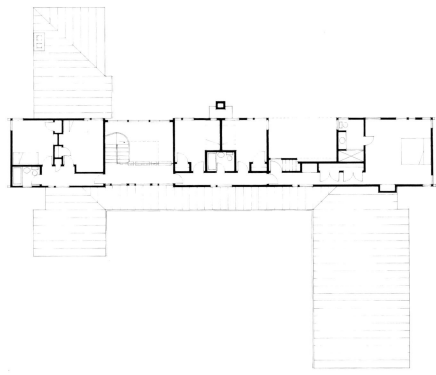

FIRST FLOOR PLAN

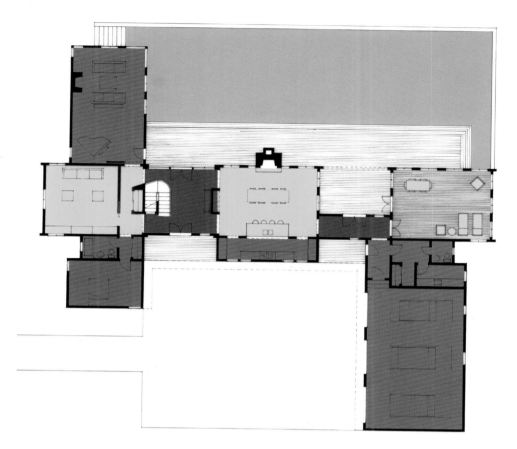

COMPUTER MODEL

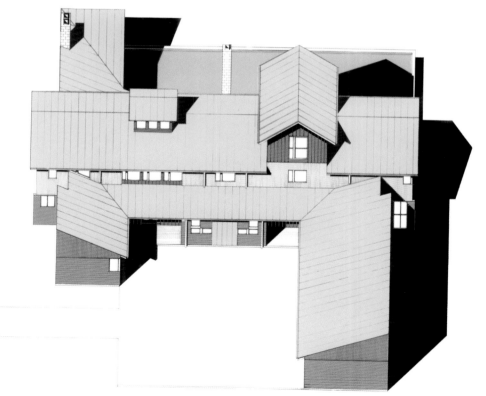

ABOVE AND LEFT: The house takes its inspiration from farm buildings and their assemblages, abstractly recalling local rural building traditions through color, form, and organization.

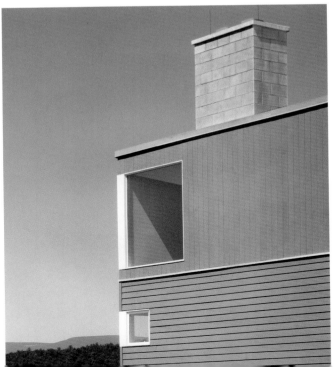

BELOW: Color is used inside and out to articulate the length of the building as three ochre pavilions with barn-red connectors.

LEFT AND ABOVE: Gray-green, shed-roofed volumes form wings, defining a terrace on the view side and a parking court on the approach side. RIGHT: A window wall floods the entry foyer with natural light.

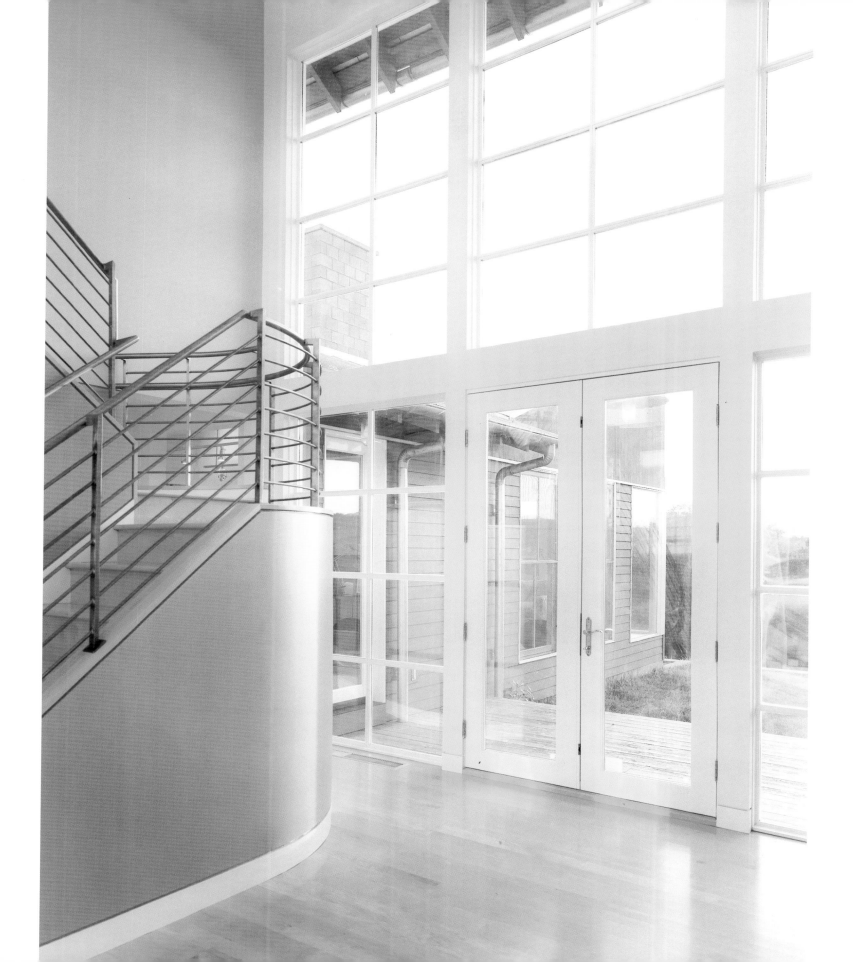

ABOVE LEFT: The dining room with concrete-block fireplace is open
to the kitchen. LEFT: The kitchen combined is with the dining area.
ABOVE: The screened porch is a third pavilion. FOLLOWING PAGES:
The porch at night has distant views of the Blue Ridge.

VINEYARD HOUSE

ARCHITECT LANE WILLIAMS ARCHITECTS
LOCATION SALEM, OREGON

A fully modern home, this remodeled vineyard farm house outside Salem, Oregon, maintains the modest gable-roofed form of the original house, and incorporates simple materials and details not typically associated with traditional farm houses.

The palette of materials is simple and straightforward, but not rustic. Traditional materials and details were replaced with a cleaner, more rugged aesthetic of poured-in-place concrete columns and fireplace, exposed fir framing, stucco walls, standing seam metal roofing, galvanized steel railings, and aluminum-framed windows.

To take advantage of the vineyard setting, the roofline was extended and large covered porches were added to the east entry façade and to the rear, west-facing façade where the owners now sit in the evening to watch the sunset.

The original house had a difficult floor plan that placed all bedrooms on the lower level; on the main level, a living-dining-area was too confined to host groups of friends and family members. To accommodate the owners' preference to live on the main level, the north end of the house was expanded to create a more spacious master bedroom suite. A new dining room was created from an existing study. The kitchen was updated and the original walnut kitchen cabinets—constructed from a single walnut tree found on the property— were preserved. The long, attic like space above the main floor received larger windows and may be used as a library and office. Original fir floors were retained, and new accents of natural stone and glass mosaic tile were added.

Now, details are geared toward understatement, all intended to create small surprises for the owners and their guests. Exposed carpentry work on exterior porches provides restrained detail. Cedar cabinets at the concrete fireplace swing open to reveal a television; a mirror floats from the wall in the master bath with a half light behind; a corner window at the soaking tub frames the sunset.

The expanded house created room for a large garage on the lower level, including an indoor kennel for two dogs whose job it is to chase deer out of the vineyard. The remainder of the lower level is devoted primarily to guest rooms and a media/game room.

New landscaping relies upon a limited range of plant material, placed in rows to recall the symmetry of the agricultural setting.

PHOTOGRAPHER LAURIE BLACK

SECOND FLOOR PLAN

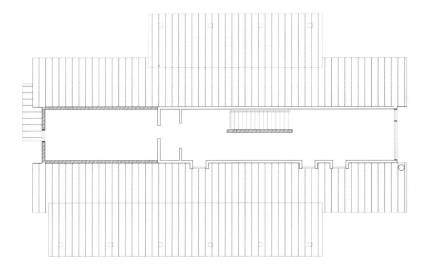

FIRST FLOOR PLAN

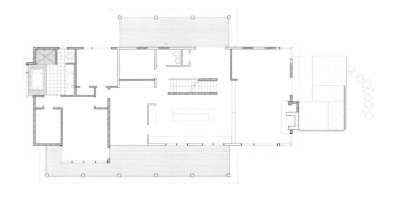

BASEMENT PLAN

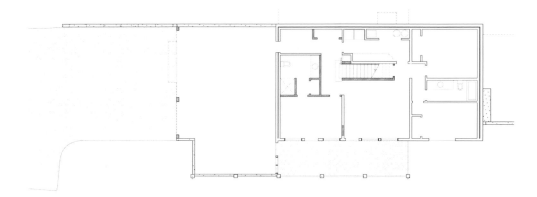

NORTH ELEVATION

SOUTH ELEVATION

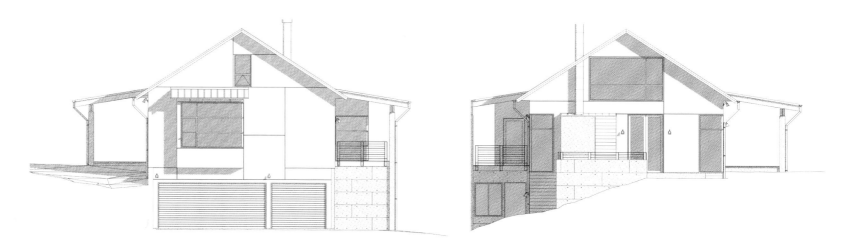

EAST ELEVATION

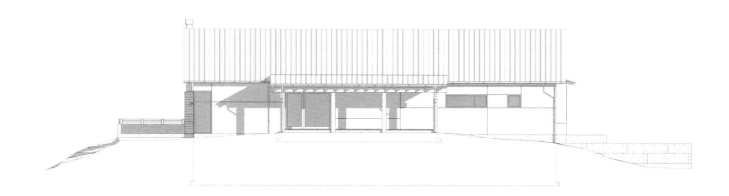

WEST ELEVATION

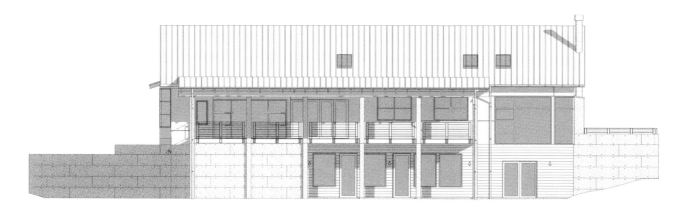

LEFT: The roofline was extended and large covered porches were
added to take advantage of views over the vineyard. BELOW: A new
concrete terrace is accessed through French doors from the living room.

ABOVE: A more rugged, contemporary aesthetic replaced the traditional materials and details of the original house. ABOVE RIGHT: The updated kitchen retains the original walnut cabinets, built from a single walnut tree found on the property. RIGHT: A new dining room was created from an existing study. FAR RIGHT: Stairs lead to a long space above the main floor that may be used as an office or study.

ABOVE: The north end of the house was expanded to create a master
bedroom suite, enabling the owners to live on the main level. RIGHT:
The bathroom features a soaking tub and views across the vineyard.

ABOVE: Entry to the house

GRASSHOPPER RANCH

ARCHITECT JOHNSTON ARCHITECTS
LOCATION METHOW VALLEY, WASHINGTON

Grasshopper Ranch sits on a bench high above the Methow River in northcentral Washington state. As ranches go, it's a fairly small 155 acres, but the hanging valley with its surrounding hills makes it feel like 1,550 acres. Few lights from other houses can be seen from the protected site; the owner is an amateur astronomer and dark skies were of utmost importance. That there was an aspen grove, a meadow, and a fabulous view was a bonus.

The client had lived in Japan, and had come to love the clean lines and the reverent use of natural materials in traditional Japanese architecture. The architects used this predilection as well as their own preference for a combination of the refined and the rural vernacular. The house pays homage to its setting not by replicating a farm house or log cabin, but by borrowing the colors of the sage and grasses, and the forms of the surrounding hills.

The house, although good sized at 3,200 square-feet, is low and long. Seen from across the valley, the house looks like a farm building of indeterminate age. Grasshopper Ranch also follows the tradition of an assembly of outbuildings surrounding the main house. For now, there is a garage with a workshop and an observatory about 40 yards from the main house. The entire roof of the small, gabled structure slides back to reveal a serious telescope that is employed by the owner most nights when there is no moon and the sky is filled with stars.

PHOTOGRAPHER STEVEN YOUNG

LOFT PLAN

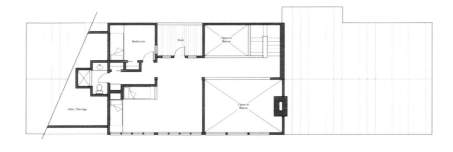

FIRST FLOOR PLAN

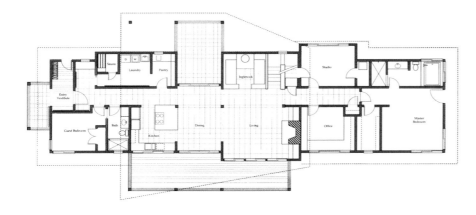

SITE PLAN

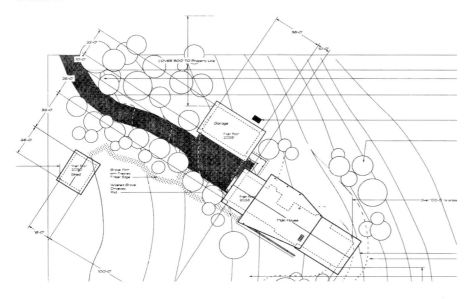

PREVIOUS PAGES: Grasshopper Ranch sits on a bench high above the Methow River in northcentral Washington state. The hanging valley with the surrounding open hills and landscape provides a rare sense of tranquility and isolation. BELOW: Having lived in Japan, the owner had come to love the clean lines and the reverent use of natural materials in traditional Japanese architecture. The architects used this predilection as well as their own preference for a combination of the refined and the rural vernacular. The house pays homage to its setting not by replicating a farm house or log cabin, but by borrowing the colors of the sage and grasses, and the forms of the surrounding hills. BELOW RIGHT: The house is low and long. Seen from across the valley, the house looks like a farm building of indeterminate age. The owner is an amateur astronomer, and dark skies were of utmost importance. That was a major consideration for siting the house. Few lights from other houses can be seen from the protected site. That there was an aspen grove, a meadow, and a fabulous view was a bonus.

LOFT PLAN

SOUTH ELEVATION

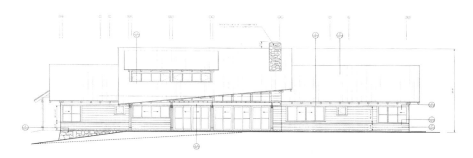

EAST ELEVATION

NORTH ELEVATION

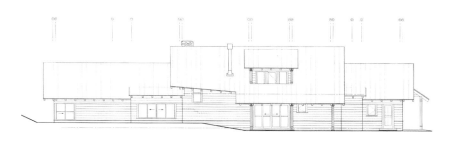

LEFT: The living room has a fieldstone fireplace, explosed beams, and second-floor loft. BELOW: Set off the living room, an inglenook creates a room within a room.

ABOVE: The dining area is open to the kitchen. RIGHT: The master bedroom has an exposed-beam ceiling. FOLLOWING PAGES: Dramatic views surround Grasshopper Ranch.

BOG CHAPEL

ARCHITECT CENTERLINE ARCHITECTS
LOCATION WOODSTOCK, VERMONT

Slightly unconventional, but very much in character with Vermont's humbler, rural architecture, this house was designed for a client who returned to the state after many years of working and traveling overseas. To create a sense of retreat, the house was located on family farmland in a low-lying area that enjoys sunlight and tranquil views of the forest and surrounding fields.

Vermont's "sugar shacks" provided the conceptual point of departure for a house that is simple and calming—a "chapel in the woods"—and at the same time, a rejection of the cookie-cutter "country mansions" that have begun to dot the surrounding hillsides. A large Coca-Cola sign placed on the exterior humorously recalls vintage commercial signs still seen on old rural buildings.

The metal shed construction evokes the surrounding agricultural setting, and the nondescript, monochromatic exterior with galvanized corrugated siding provides no hint of the contemporary plan inside. The cross-gable plan works well, minimizing circulation, with all spaces connecting from a central main room that includes sitting and dining areas. A private master bedroom suite and office are situated off the main room. Large, sliding French doors from the main room open to a spacious screened porch that during warm weather serves as an extension to the main room. The upstairs is planned to accommodate guests and provide privacy. Two bedrooms open to a sitting room with a separate, second-floor screened porch.

Very simple materials and construction techniques characterize this house. Bright, saturated color—inspired by the owner's time spent in Latin America—is used on the interior walls throughout the house.

Environmental features used in the house include a southern exposure, renewable materials, high insulation values, radiant floor heat, and low-flow toilets and showerheads. Native plants were used extensively in the landscaping.

PHOTOGRAPHER MARK CHANEY

ATTIC PLAN

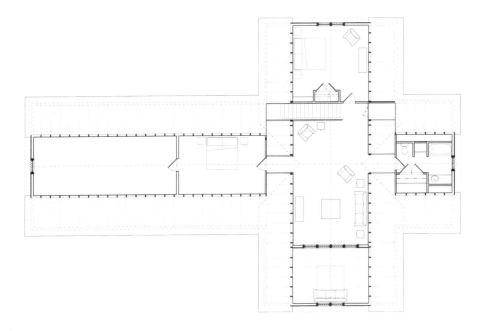

PREVIOUS PAGES: This unconventional house was inspired by Vermont's "sugar shacks." The shed construction and corrugated galvanized metal siding provide no hint of the contemporary plan inside. The decorative Coca-Cola sign recalls the old metal signs often seen on rural buildings.

SITE PLAN

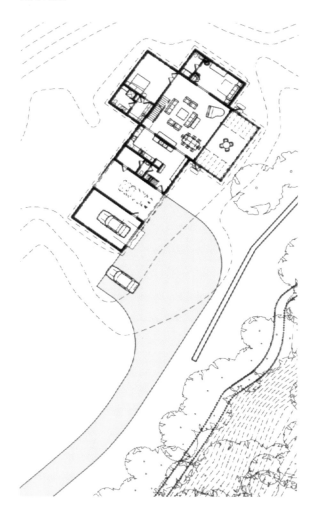

FIRST FLOOR PLAN

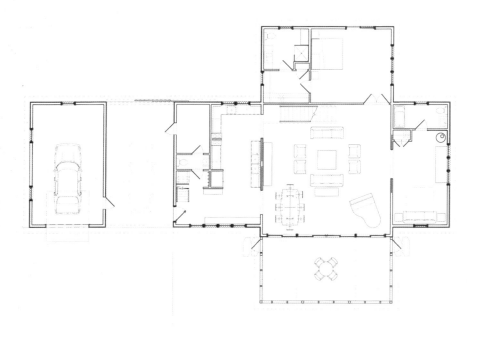

ELEVATION

ELEVATION

ELEVATION

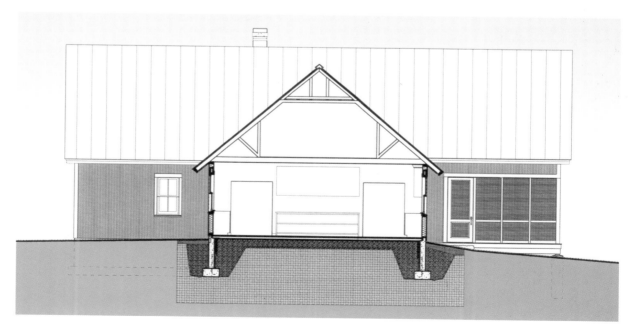

LEFT AND ABOVE: The house serves as a retreat, located on farmland in a sunny, low-lying area surrounded by meadows and forest. RIGHT: A large screened porch serves as an extension to the main room inside.

ABOVE AND ABOVE RIGHT: The cross-gable plan minimizes circulation, as all public spaces connect from a central main room. A private master bedroom suite and office are situated off the main room. Large sliding French doors lead to the screened porch.

ABOVE: Deep, saturated color brightens the modern kitchen.

ABOVE LEFT: The staircase leads to private guest rooms upstairs.
ABOVE: Interior colors are inspired by the owner's time spent in
Latin America.

ARCHITECTS

Rivera Barn
The Dahlin Group Architecture Planning
2671 Crow Canyon Road
San Ramon, CA 94583
Tel. 925.837.8286
www.dahlingroup.com

Wagner Residence
Wagner McCann Studio Landscape Architects
7 Marble Avenue
Burlington, VT 05401
Tel. 802.864.0010
www.wagnermccannstudio.com
and
Birdseye Building Company
3104 Huntington Road
Richmond, VT 05477
Tel. 802.434.2112 ext. 13
www.birdseyebuilding.com

Jones Farmstead
Salmela Architecture and Design
852 Grandview Avenue
Duluth, MN 55812
Tel. 218.724.7517
www.salmelaarchitect.com

Little Big House
Shipley Architects
4438 Dyer St. #107
Dallas, TX 75206
Tel. 214.823.2080
www.shipleyarchitects.com

Chauvin Farm House
Holly and Smith Architects
208 North Cate Street
Hammond, LA 70401
Tel. 985.345.5210
www.hollyandsmith.com

Napa Farm House
Osborn Design Group
822 D. College Avenue
Santa Rosa, CA 95404
Tel. 707.542.3770
www.osborndesigngroup.com

Mad Architecture
145 Keller Street
Petaluma,CA 94952
Tel. 707.765.9222
www.majouc.com

Dog Trot House
Waggonner & Ball Architects
2200 Prytania Street
New Orleans, LA 70130
Tel. 504.524.5308
www.wbarchitects.com

Coastal Retreat
Aidlin Darling Design
500 Third Street, Suite 410
San Francisco, CA 94107
Tel. 415.974.5603
www.aidlin-darling-design.com

Holmes Farmstead
Salmela Architecture and Design
852 Grandview Avenue
Duluth, MN 55812
Tel. 218.724.7517
www.salmelaarchitect.com

Freeman House
SALA Architects, Inc.
43 Main Street, SE, Suite 410
Minneapolis, MN 55414
Tel. 612.379.3037
www.salaarc.com

Wild Hair
Mell Lawrence Architects
913 W. Gibson
Austin, TX 78704
Tel. 512.441.4669
www.architecturalpolka.com

Scrabbletown House
Durkee, Brown, Viveiros & Werenfels Architects
300 West Exchange Street
Providence, RI 02903
Tel. 401.831.1240
www.durkeebrown.com

Bucks County Home
Donald Billinkoff Architects
310 Riverside Drive, Suite 202-1
New York, NY 10025
Tel. 212.678.7755
www.billinkoff.com

Rappahannock House
McInturff Architects
4220 Leeward Place
Bethesda, MD 20816
Tel. 301.229.3705
www.mcinturffarchitects.com

Vineyard House
Lane Williams Architects
327 Second Avenue West
Seattle, WA 98119
Tel. 206.284.8355
www.lanewilliams.com

Grasshopper Ranch
Johnston Architects
3503 NE 45th Street, Suite 2
Seattle, WA 98105
Tel. 206.523.6150
www.johnstonarchitects.com

Bog Chapel
Centerline Architects
302 Main Street
Bennington, VT 05201
Tel. 802.447.8609
www.clarch.com